BOOK 1

W9-AVA-223

Grand SOLOS FOR Piano

10 PIECES FOR EARLY ELEMENTARY PIANISTS
WITH OPTIONAL DUET ACCOMPANIMENTS

Melody Bober

When I was a young piano student, nothing thrilled me more than receiving a new piano solo from my teacher. It was always something unique and challenging, yet fun to practice and perform.

Students today are no different; new music is still fun and exciting to receive. In that spirit, I have written *Grand Solos for Piano*, Book 1, to provide the same experience for today's performers. This collection contains music in a variety of keys, styles, meters and tempos, offering students a great learning experience as well as helping them progress technically and musically. In addition, each piece includes an optional duet accompaniment for teacher, parents or other family members to share in the fun.

I sincerely hope that you will enjoy these *Grand Solos for Piano*!

Best wishes,

CONTENTS

ISBN-10: 0-7390-5198-9
ISBN-13: 978-7390-5198-6

Alfred

Summer Afternoon

Melody Bober

DUET ACCOMPANIMENT: Student plays one octave higher.

* No pedal when played with duet accompaniment.

Blarney Stone Jig

Melody Bober

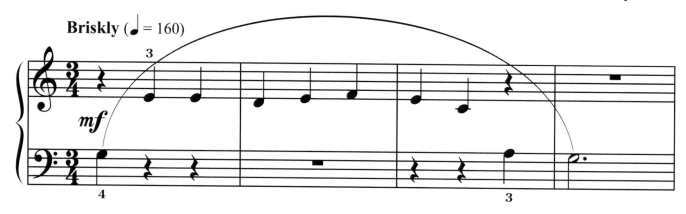

DUET ACCOMPANIMENT: Student plays one octave higher.

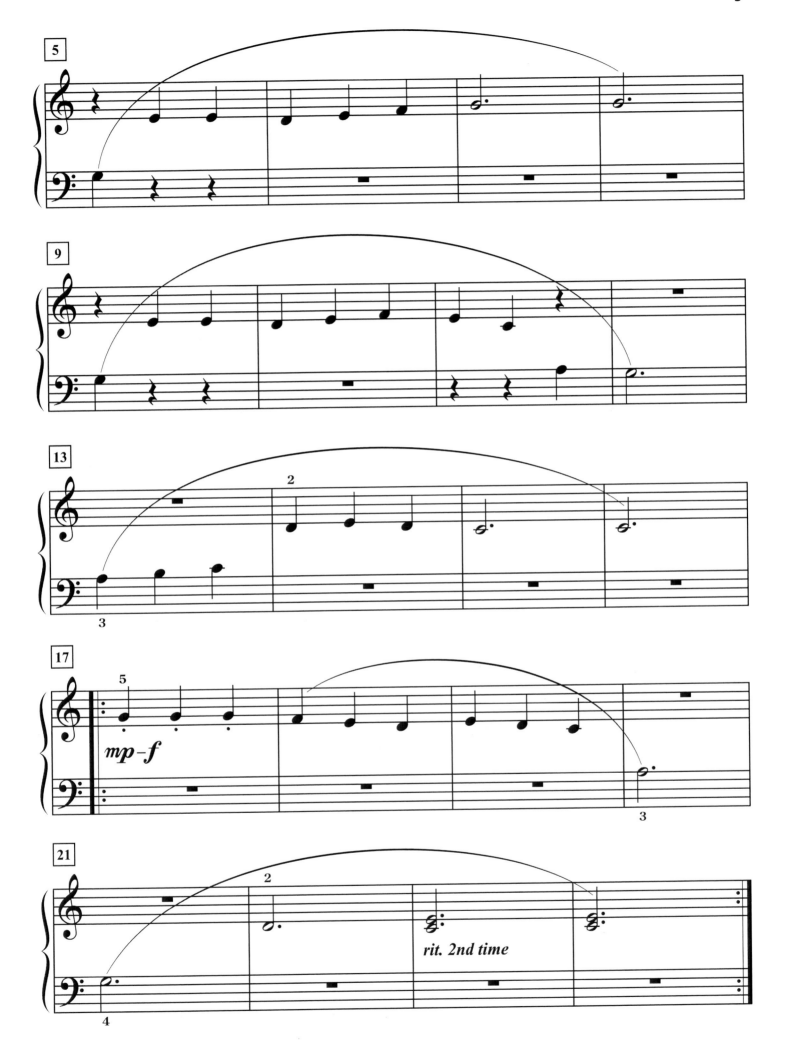

6

Sneakin' Around

Melody Bober

DUET ACCOMPANIMENT: Student plays one octave higher.

Commissioned by the Piano Pedagogy Lab School at
Washington State University, Pullman, Washington

College Hill Cheer

Melody Bober

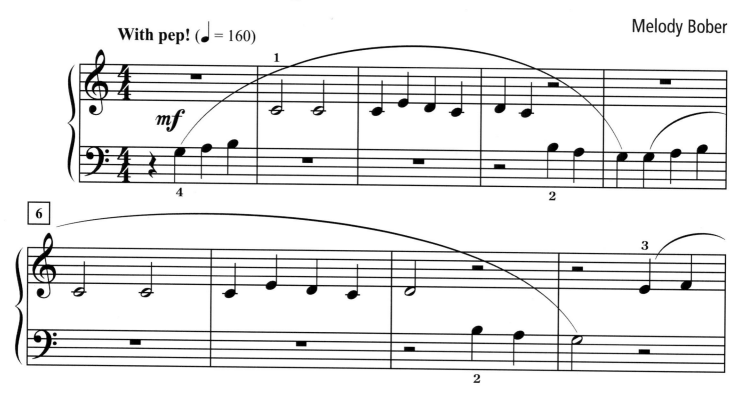

DUET ACCOMPANIMENT: Student plays one octave higher.

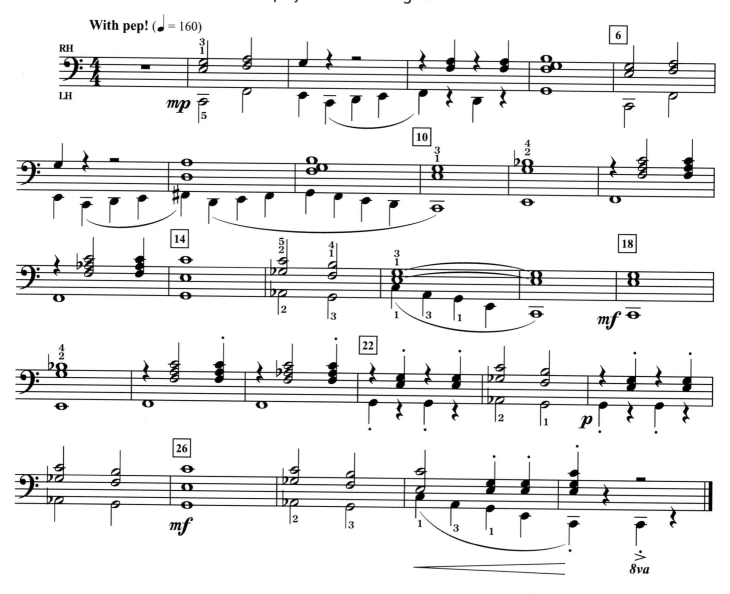

Black Cat Waltz

Melody Bober

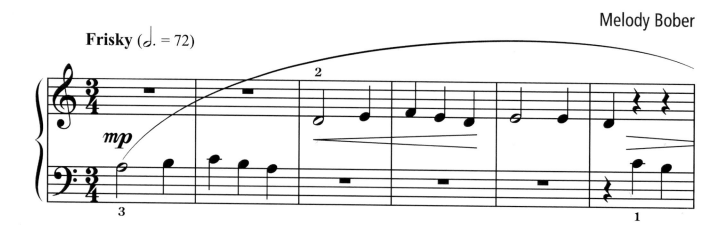

DUET ACCOMPANIMENT: Student plays one octave higher.

Snowboard Boogie

Melody Bober

DUET ACCOMPANIMENT: Student plays one octave higher.

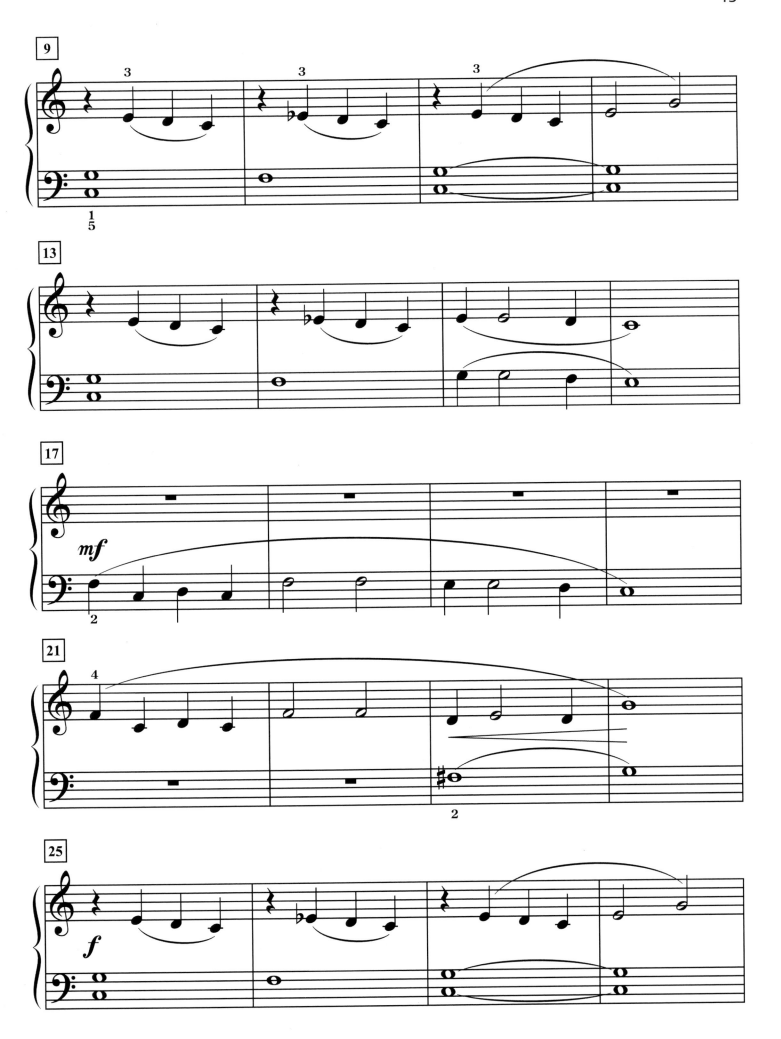

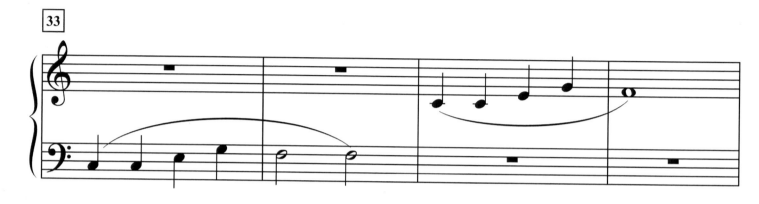

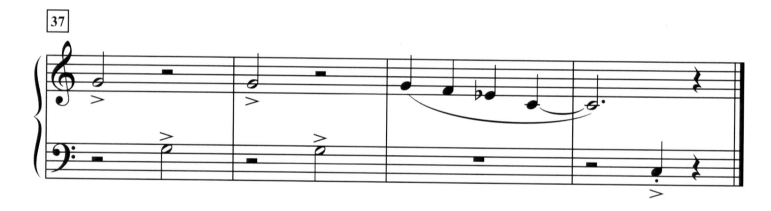

DUET ACCOMPANIMENT *(continued)*

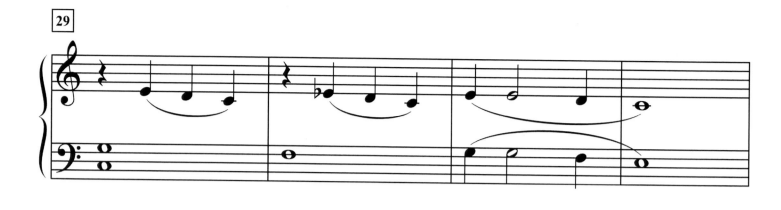

Tiptoe in the Dark

Melody Bober

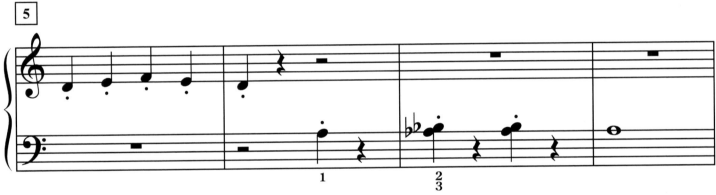

DUET ACCOMPANIMENT: Student plays one octave higher.

DUET ACCOMPANIMENT *(continued)*

Sea Song

Melody Bober

DUET ACCOMPANIMENT: Student plays one octave higher.

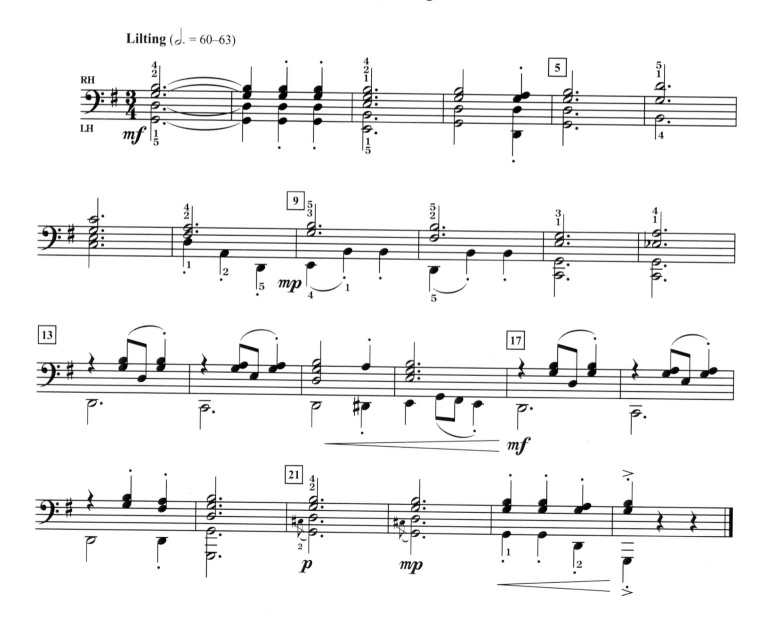

A Frightful Night

Melody Bober

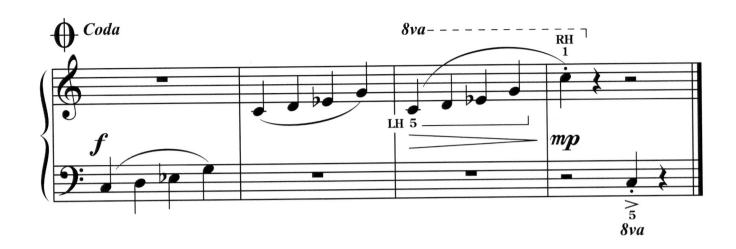

DUET ACCOMPANIMENT: Student plays one octave lower.

Magic Maracas

Melody Bober

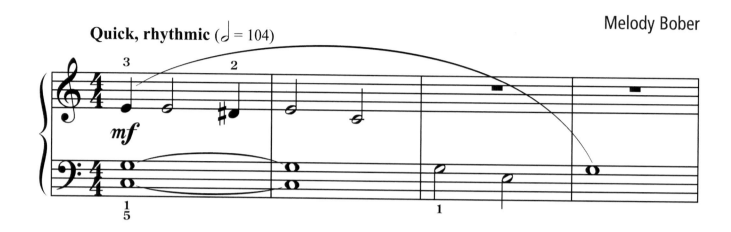

DUET ACCOMPANIMENT: Student plays one octave higher.

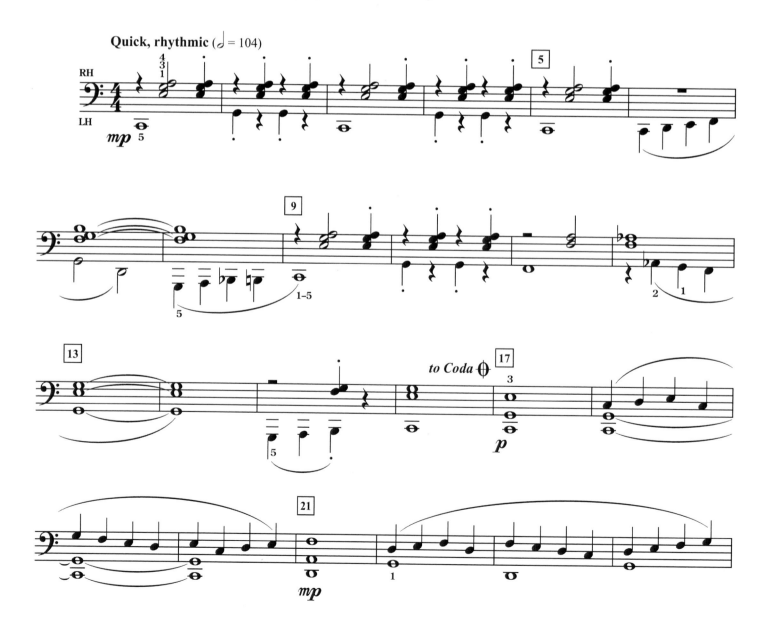

to Coda

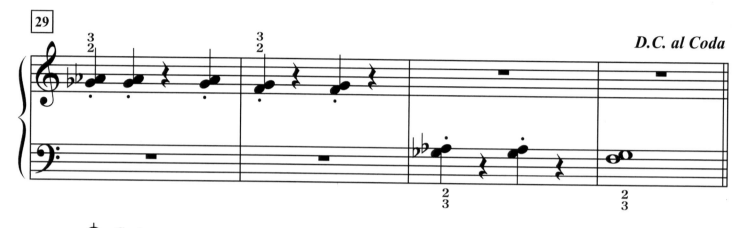

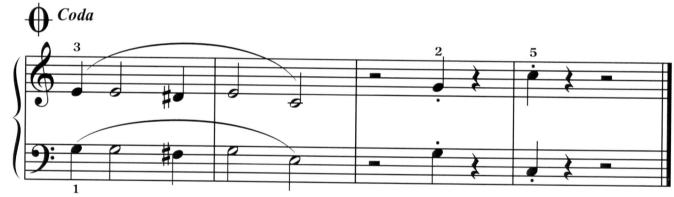

DUET ACCOMPANIMENT (continued)

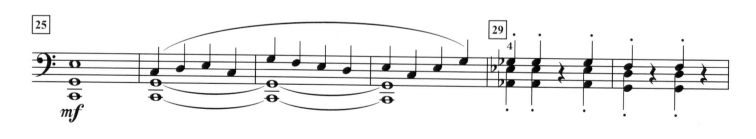

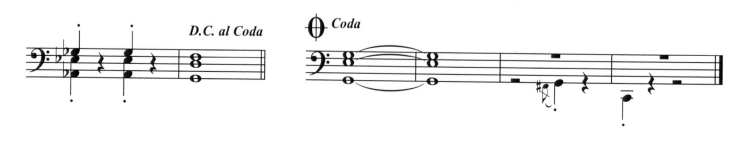